POEMS FROM MOUNTMELLICK

Poems from Mountmellick

Copyright © 2021 by John Lawlor

All rights reserved. No part of this book may be reproduced in any manner whatsoever without written permission except in the case of educational studies such as quotes, or brief quotations embodied in critical articles and reviews.

First Printing, 2021

≈ 1 ≈

THE FACES IN THE BOOK

Lost in the moment to a different time
Waiting for soup in an orderly line

The scars of battle from the streets six a side
"We all come from Davin Park", the glory, the pride

That eerie lane was our shortcut to play
We'd be there all the time once it hit may

Bikes abandoned all over the place
Held together with twine and shoe lace

Swapping stickers, "who do you need"
Just one more gold one and I'll be in the lead

Offside didn't exist and fly goalie was quick
And goalposts were either a jumper or a stick

Smiths field is still there, in our wonderful town
The focal point of friendship, safe and sound

Right now when I'm looking back at this tattered schoolbook
Scrolling back and forward … This is my Face Book

≈ 2 ≈
A GOOD STRETCH OF THE LEG

Summer time and the old rust bike is going hell for leather

Determined to meet up with the lads whatever the weather

Weighed down with frozen drinks to quench the thirst

We head down to Stoney Dempseys first

A mad notion and we end up in the Cinder Hills

I think we took a wrong turn in the New Mills

As we stopped to collect nuts growing wild

Before we knew it we were in Derryguile

We couldn't believe our look when we found a few pound

And rushed to Dick and Jims ... Two abreast through the town

Our last big adventure was to conquer the famous river banks

For all our memories and blisters

... To our hometown ...

Thanks

3

LOOKING FOR DIRECTIONS

Excuse me sir, I was wondering, where I can find
Where the heart of this grand town intertwines

Well sir, pleased to meet you, it use to be here
Where I started my run and picked up my gear

Sure everything changed in the blink of an eye
Are you having me on? Where's the best place for a fry

Everything's here, all on one street
It's not too busy these days, one time they were run off their feet

Will you hold that mug steady for me? I've a shake in me hand
I know the feeling, no bother, you'll be grand

You see, my family lived here, before they set sail
I can fondly remember, lovely scenic photos in our mail

They proudly mentioned the friendly banter and smiles
And the céad mile fáilte at the seat in Derryguile

Not to forget their very own fear an post delivering a tune
When he stops for a break beside the well in Garoon

It was a pleasure to meet you, please enjoy your stay
You know the old saying "when the sun shines, make hay

The turf needs footing, I'll be up half the night
And it's a job and a half keeping the spudz safe from blight

4

BACK IN THE DAY

Guns and holsters, bikes without helmets
Headers and volleys, fly goalies and tennis

Marking out pitches "give me back me ball"
Halloween pranks, goalposts in the hall

Whiskey bottles for minnows, steppingstones,
great camping spots

Robbing paradise orchard, peg guns and sling shots

D.I.Y. go carts, nut and bolt bangers
5p for dew bottles, tellies with hangers

Water on freezing paths, slipping and sliding
Ringing doorbells, running and hiding

Carnival tent wettings, the old man hiding the guns
Sports day in the green, long jumps and sprint runs

Cloghies was the place for loose fags and chocolate mice

Save all your pennies 'great pair of boys'
The billiard hall on a Sunday, "who said mass?"

The steel structure in the square, still there, built to last

DAYDREAMING

Hypnotised from the tick tock ... Tick tock on the wall
Out for the count into dreamland I fall

Summer has finally arrived, I'm hoping
Rushing to the door with laces half open

Cherry blossoms cover wheel and feet
The freedom of the open road is hard to beat

Can't wait to get home and abandon the books
To a carefree world and not give two fecks

The old potholed lane awaits my trusty black rothar
Leaving dust behind, burning rubber

The well-worn track leading to Stoney's uisce of blue
A hidden gem, only known by the chosen few

A 5.30 start has my young heart broken
Time for the bog, with eyes barely open

Cold water from the fountain at the top of the bay
Wakes me up and sets me up for the day

Carefully footing the wet peat, a thought enters my mind
Of another generation in a different time

Two worlds collide as the dew starts to fall
Awoken by the hour bell and I'm back in the school hall

UP AT THE CRACK OF DAWN

The perfect square of earthly clod
"Nice day" ... Lovely, thank God

Love the colour, which one, oh...the green
Mixed it myself ... Goes nice with the cream

The blue and white is lovely on the well
Ye ... UP LAOIS ... Hopefully, an end to the dry spell

What's the bog like, were you up there at all
There's a great crust but no wind at all

Wasn't that a fierce long winter this year
Never saw it as bad in all my 80 years

Did you spray for the blight or did you bother
I used a homemade mix, handed down by my late mother

Can't really use the sprayer, my hands are in a bad way
The auld arthritis ... Will you have some tae?

There's a flask inside ... Work away
Hard to believe it's the 21st ... The longest day

It's all downhill from here ... Where does time go at all
Talking of which ... I may head on, don't forget your package on the wall

Well done ... Saw you on this weeks paper
It was a good bit of craic ... Nice chatting ... God bless ...
See you later

ng postman in online film

...man John Lawlor is the star of a YouTube video made by local videographer John Lynch.

...one to film it. It was recorded around Christmas so it was great to get the Christmas lights around... switched on," said Lawlor.

"...postman's job has changed "big time" over the... he said.

...go to the Portlaoise mail centre to sort the post every morning, that's a big change. One time we had pigeon holes now it's all up to date," he said.

"People still send plenty of letters," he said, with "five times as much post at Christmas...

...part now but we deliver smaller packets. People post letters and those ways to bills," he said.

"I hope to be doing post for the next... working life," Lawlor said.

THE KNOCK AT THE DOOR

I often sat and wondered
When he waved goodbye at the manor gate

How his grief stricken mother
Learned of his cruel fate

As a child we heard some great stories
But I couldn't understand

Why there was no headstone
No flowers, nothing special, nothing grand

Was there even an act of contrition?
Whispered in his ear

Was there any final wishes?
Did he suffer? did he fear?

A long time has passed now
And I finally comprehend

Why in those times, he was just another statistic
For the Green, White and Gold of Ireland

We will never forget our dear soldier brave
whose life for the cause he proudly gave

BRIGHTER DAYS WILL COME

There's an eeriness in the valley ... Everywhere is closed

The only sound you can hear is when the cock crows

The echo from pounding pavements has evaporated in the early morning mist

And the friendly schoolkid banter is on a temporary waiting list

Business as usual as the bills land on the ground

A lovely singing voice belts out melody all around

"What's the craic" from an open window

If there's anything you need, just let me know

An elderly lady thanks me for all the work we do

With a heartfelt thumbs up, completely out of the blue

Scary times are with us, but we'll answer Irelands call

We will get through this, all for one and one for all

THE COLD NOVEMBER RAIN

Sad reflection, glassy eyes
Rippling water, fearful noise

Panic stations in Mountmellick town
But floating through, a new friend I found

"Have you time for tae or maybe a beer"
Stories about yesteryear

Capturing the moment, "what's that thing ... Something face"
Phone cameras all over the place

Enjoying the chat, time to head for the hills
For a moment there, time stood still

Community spirit with no abound
Neighbours and friends rally around

Back to reality
That soul destroying rain

But don't forget that old wise man's words
"THE VALLEY WILL RISE AGAIN"

Subsided river under hollow banks
Generous donations, fair play, thanks

Recharged batteries, thank God, no more sand
Upwards and onwards, new hope, new plans

A tug of war against the elements, stretched full
A rope, artistically decorated with one big heart ... Inspired by wool

≈ 10 ≈

SMALL TOWN BIG HEART

Generations of happy memories, engraved on golden leaves, all blown and scattered

And form the perfect sign, all across its famous crib … "Our tree matters"

The mighty steel structure sways to the rhythm of new life, new plans, wow … What a rallying call

Everyone digging deep, all for one and one for all

The changing times will never change our people

Proud generations stand as proud as the steeple

Young lads on sturdy bikes leggin it up town to give a hand

Let's meet up at the tree … That's the plan

Upwards and onwards, for our famous Christmas tree

And the best of luck to both the old and new volunteer committee!

≈ 11 ≈
DARKNESS INTO LIGHT

Transformed with wild Irish beauty

Fragrant drooping petals hang delicately in springs gentle feathered breeze
As I tip toe through violet blue heaven ... Take it all in and breathe

Wildlife sticks to glossy green like glue
Sun light reflects fragrance, gleaming effortlessly beyond our valley's sea of blue

Rainbow colours contrast with close family, pink and white relations
Finally spring awakens April from its annual hibernation

The once abandoned woodland has been
flower bombed overnight

≈ 12 ≈
THE BARK ON THE AEROPLANE TREE

Old Irish pennies catch my eye at a glance

Golden trumpets seem lost in her trance

Magic wings propelled by springs gentle breeze

The sabhaircín hides your front door keys

The first rose leads to Tír Na Nógs mystical land of dream

Dew droplets glisten on botanical perennial green

Crunching footprints, energetic misty breath

Belief in tomorrow, peeping tete a tete

Galanthus nivalis, oblique heavenly bed

Perfect octave 'till sundown fade'

≈ 13 ≈

CYCLE FOR LEUKAEMIA

A child reaches out and my soul is touched
Putting everything in to perspective ... life is tough
Still he smiles at a robin who lands in my hand
And sings a sad song ... Only he can understand

Trapped in a relentless bubble of pain
His life is one hell of a migraine
I hear his cry for help in this hard auld station
As he waits patiently for bone marrow donation

Don't worry, together, we will see this through
Don't be down, don't sing the blues
Blossoms of Hope fall from Aprils cherry trees

With everyone's help ...
Keep up the good work and donate ... Please

We are all a link in the fundraising bike
Thanks for all the shares and likes

Samhain

On this all souls eve a bright candle shines

To remember loved ones and precious times

To dream and chat with sad empty yearn

At the hearths peat fire ... They are remembered in song

I've reached so deep with empty solace

Till darkness fades into tomorrow

≈ 15 ≈
DISTRACTED BY AN ANGEL

Walking by, stopping to say hello

Merry Christmas … Ho Ho Ho

Trying to tell me something, but I can't understand

As we chat and shake hands

His teary eyes are focused on the holly tree

At something only he can see

All of a sudden a lullaby he starts to sing

And a robin lands beside us with a broken wing

It was a lonely time for the sick child in the pram

Who was pointing at the brightest star … His mam

≈ 16 ≈
DIG IN

Drifting off …. Dreaming of mothers cabbage and Bacona
Ricochet from the parapet
Another mate taken
Overcoats stuck to frost hardened snow
Numb tingled hand and toe

Red streams and rodents
The fear of no way out
"10 rounds rapid fire"
Pass on the message **"shout!"**
No man's rock hard land
Time to advance
Fumbling for bayonets
"This is it … Adopt the stance"

Panic spreads rapidly
Gas everywhere, gasp for air through blurred eyes
One by one, young comrades drop like flies
Reality sets in on our great adventure
The stench of death awakens me
Damn this shellshock
It's the flashbacks again sir

≈ 17 ≈
THE SINGERS LAMENT

With the click of a finger life's ingredients rise to the top

In a heartbeat the oven goes cold and the cake will flop

The parting glass celebrates at short journeys end

Spilling over and stirred with poetic pen

I cannot stay, to see the spudz turning red

I've grown weary in gardens sun bed

Fill my empty drills with strong tenors voice

I've loved the craic, it was inspirational, it was really, really nice

≈ 18 ≈

SHATTERED BUT NOT BROKEN

The stage was set, everything planned

Their fate was met, dealt a cruel hand

Into the semi's, everything to gain

When all of a sudden, panic entered the plane

It failed to take off and came to a stall

The dream was over for European football

But they rallied together at this difficult time

Young, ambitious players, cut down in their prime

We sing their praises and remember in prayer

Sixty-two years later
"THE FLOWERS OF MANCHESTER"

It's something which comes from deep in the heart

Our journey didn't end...it was only the start

19

THE BLACK SHEEP

As I return to the first chapter in life's dusty page
The grandfather clock never lost a second in old age

Framed on whitewashed walls, a faded photo
A young soldier's medals and promotion

And the fear an phoist belting out little dark rose róisín

Smoke filled laughter reaches the sky
From the heart of an open fire with turf piled high

Chatting away with perfect silver hair and mittens, trembling hands
She could make that squeezebox talk, could mam

Oh here's my king of hearts
Let's dance you smile and say

Just like the good old days
The thatched roof is locked in a time capsule

Childhood memories of pockets full of sticky sweets at school
The hour bell has robbed your senses but not your heart of gold

I'm weary of travelling and have returned to the fold

≈ 20 ≈
A STICH IN TIME

Special memories bloom with love and hugs

Pride of place in a special mug

The hour bell has tried to rob my favourite rose

But it's got better with time ... And still glows

Hard times mended with silver threads and hugs

A kiss on the forehead and everything is good

Turning back the caring hands of life's clock to cradles start

And listen to lullabies sung straight from her heart

"If only"

AN IRISH CELEBRATION

No lavish food, just bread and milk

To welcome Mary and Joseph ... The season of goodwill

A light in the largest window to guide them at night

Under nollaig shona, joyful and bright

Treats for the big man with the rosy glow

Turf fires burning and plenty of snow

12 pubs, 12 days and a freezing festive swim

Frosted front doors decorated with holly rings

The lovely midnight choir send a shiver through the crowd

Parents watching school concerts, patiently and proud

Dressed up wren boys with not a note in our heads

Twas great craic though and a few bob was made

22

LOCKED UP AND LOCKED DOWN

Panic buying, empty shelves and lonely souls

Worried kids, playing obliviously on gaming consoles

If only the remote control could unlock reality

Yes, Eire is emerald green and her sunny sky is blue and clear

Her roads are unusually Quiet for this time of the year

Everywhere is painted and all the paths are clear

A time to reflect, doze off and dream

Neighbours sing to each other from afar

No handshakes … Grandparents broken hearts

Kisses tearily blown from fogged up windows

But still her shamrock glistens and grows

The spirit of her native Gael still flows

With a' Dia Duit' and shake of elbows

This horrible, horrible, springtime of year

Is cursed and followed by covids dark cloud of fear

≈ 23 ≈
THE DAY THE MUSIC DIED

The chorus embraces joyful lament
Its audience are captivated with cryptic content
Heartfelt applause through clenched teary eyes
Calmness in darkened thoughts from musical disguise

Life is the heartbeat in musical chords
We are just the instruments, belting out the words
The lyrics are composed from deep within your soul
Until you run our of aces and it's time to fold

The music yearns for passion and heart
But grey clouds start lashing ... It's time to part
Farewell my friend, my only friend, sorrowful goodbyes
Nothing lasts forever, even the music dies

Enter the cold and try to be brave
Gently fold, kind-hearted, engraved
We held fingers at cradle, now hold hands at grave
Bound tightly forever through musical octave

OPENING A DRILL

Calloused hands on painted surface

Uneven drills, staggered on purpose

The perfect sod, layered by rusty spade

Golden trumpets dance and fade

Melody echoes through a robins friendly chime

All that's left from last years crop is parsley and thyme

The drills are open so the fun can begin

Tradition dictates, the youngest puts the first spud in

My trusty tin whistle is never silent for long

As I stop for a break and ponder a song

Where does the time go at all, it's nearly time for the tae

Jack Frost is starting to bite, so I'll bid you good day

RAY OF HOPE

Welcome back ... Summer's golden cherry warm smile

Cold spade waits for you in lonely compost pile

Nothing is guaranteed ... Except the start and the end

The hour bell waits around every corner and every bend

The abandoned long road will bloom with wild delight

At last, Heaven's carpet of Irish bluebells transforms

DARKNESS INTO LIGHT

A GRAND STRETCH

So it's here at last … Hip hip hooray

Let's raise a glass to the shortest day

Spring motivates the restless gardener out of his comfy bed

To measure out and plan ahead

Like an artist, blending colour with shade

As he checks the clay with rusty spade

Time has given him love and love has given him time

A mix and match of spring and summer sublime

All his wisdom is stored beneath cabbage and cauliflower

Just bursting to escape the longest hour

Soon trumpets will dance with merry heart

Goodbye long nights … Welcome brighter starts

CHRISTMAS REFLECTION 2020

'Twas Christmas eve night just before lockdown
There was a great session goin .... Singing, rocking around
The windows were open, decorations and holly blowing
Santy was on the way and the excitement was growing
Everything was cleaned, even the chimney was 'Sanitized'
Just like in the song ... We checked it twice
Nostalgic memories, annual traditions
Party pieces, poems, trad music and renditions
A toast to remember our deer loved ones who passed
As we look forward to celebrate socially distanced mass
We pray for all the front-line workers
'Thank you and keep safe!'
You're heart and soul willingly and caringly you give
Covid will slow us down for a while, but we won't give up the fight
Just like our brave kin who battled famine and blight

HEAVEN SCENT

So it's here at last ... Hip hip hooray

Peeping from lonely abandoned homestead

Escaping a sacred freezing bed

Scattered in clumps of Heavens White Carpet

Hypnotising me with mystical charm and shivering me with regret

The first time of bloom left me sad at heart

A constant reminder why young love left, before it could start

But still you keep your promise to always be around

Soon you'll die again and return to earths cold ground

≈ 29 ≈
FLOWER OF HOPE

Shivering through melting snow from head to feet

Spring awakens tough blossom from deep sleep

A precious gift from heaven in pure form

On this December day when the saviour is born

STAYCATION

Heading back to my home town where my heart belongs

To stroll along the river banks, it's scenery and sounds

Like the perfection of a finely tuned song

In awe of unique ripple as it hugs and golden sun smiles

An artists view of the best place in the world, by a mile

I have missed the blue and white of my happy childhood, of my life start

Where it's fine folk have the gift of the gab down to a fine art

At the drop of a hat, great banter and song

Even though half of the lyrics might be wrong

Some lads even add in a verse or three

The secret to a good session is good monteach tea

So, if you're passing by, Whether young or old

The stove is warm with local reared turf stacked high

Welcome, put your feet up, come in out of the cold

MEET THE AUTHOR

JOHN LAWLOR

John is an Irish poet from the town of Mountmellick in County Laois in Ireland, 1 of 5 brothers John spent his younger years in and around the countryside town getting up to mischief with the boys all over the place, some of these antics are the foundation for some of his poems. He became the local postman of the town and built a reputation as the 'Singing Postman' even featuring in a short documentary.

His love of poetry and creative writing can be found all the way back to his youth when he wrote his poem, 'THE SINGERS LAMENT', since then he has developed his poetry into a diverse outlook on the world.

Known for being a generous individual this filters right down to his poetry, donating his profits to local charities in his hometown which he loves so much, one of the fundraisers which is very dear to his heart is the focus of a poem called, 'CYCLE FOR LEUKAEMIA', in which John poetically brings the readers attention to the much needed help and support for children suffering from illnesses like this.

John is currently working on new material that he hopes to also have published and to donate the profits to more charitable causes. His family and the community in which he grew up in, are immensely proud of John, his character he brings to his 'Small Town with a Big Heart'.